SACRAMENTO PUBLIC LIBRARY
8
SACR
D0565772

ZOMBIE FELTIES

How to raise 16 gruesome felt creatures from the undead

Nicola Tedman & Sarah Skeate

**Andrews McMeel
Publishing, LLC**

Kansas City • Sydney • London

Zombie Felties

Copyright © 2010 by Ivy Press Limited

All rights reserved. No part of this book may be used or reproduced in any manner whatsoever without written permission except in the case of reprints in the context of reviews. For information, write to:
ANDREWS McMEEL PUBLISHING, LLC
an Andrews McMeel Universal company
1130 Walnut Street
Kansas City, Missouri 64106

www.andrewsmcmeel.com

ISBN: 978-0-7407-9764-4

This book was conceived, designed, and produced by:
Ivy Press
210 High Street, Lewes
East Sussex BN7 2NS, UK
www.ivy-group.co.uk

Creative Director Peter Bridgewater
Publisher Jason Hook
Editorial Director Tom Kitch
Commissioning Editor Sophie Collins
Senior Designer Kate Haynes
Designer Joanna Clinch
Illustrator Melvyn Evans
Photographer Andrew Perris

Printed in China
Color origination by Ivy Press Reprographics

10 11 12 13 14 IYP 12 11 10 9 8 7 6 5 4 3 2

Important!
Safety warning: Zombie felties are not toys.
Many have small, removable parts and should
be kept out of the reach of small children.

CONTENTS

STARTING OUT

How to make sure your zombies look good

Despite their horrid appearance, Zombie Felties are quite easy to sew provided that you follow a few simple guidelines and pointers for making your first one or two. Be warned, though, not only are these zombies far too unsettling for small children to play with, but most also have plenty of sharp or tiny detachable pieces.

TOOLS

Use sharp scissors for cutting and snipping, and use the smallest embroidery needle you're comfortable with to add details and sew the felties together.

The craft glue that comes in a tube with a tiny nozzle dispenser is easiest to use; alternatively, use a glue stick and, when glue is needed for a very small area, scrape a bit off and use the point of a needle, matchstick, or toothpick to apply it accurately.

A disappearing marking pen is best for drawing around templates. These are popular with quilters and are available at most craft stores. They draw a line on fabric that simply disappears after a few days. You can also use it to mark out stitching or placement for adding details on the felt pieces.

TEMPLATES

You can scan and print or photocopy the pattern pieces on the template pages at 100 percent, then simply cut them out. If you don't have easy access to a scanner and printer or photocopier, trace the pattern pieces for the zombie you want to make onto tracing paper with a soft pencil. All the templates in the book are the correct size to make the zombies shown; none of them will need scaling up or down.

STUFFING THE ZOMBIES

Use a customized toy stuffing to fill your zombies: It is light, and it's also easy to separate out the minute wisps for stuffing the dolls. Don't be tempted to use cotton balls or batting instead—they'll clump and make for a lumpy little doll. Use something small and pointed—we suggest a matchstick or pointed tweezers—to help you distribute the stuffing evenly in the tinier pieces.

SEWING AND EMBROIDERY

All the zombies are both embroidered and stitched together with embroidery floss. Standard floss comes in a small skein, with thread made up of six separate strands. You can pull the floss apart to get the thickness specified in the patterns. You'll find that the floss is used in single or double threads in most of the instructions, although more strands will occasionally be called for in specific patterns or stitches. To get the number of threads you want, cut a short length of floss, around 12–16 inches (30–40 cm) long, and simply separate the desired number of strands from the main piece, pulling gently from one end. Keep the other strands to use elsewhere. To secure the thread, either tie a small knot at the end of the floss, or make a tiny cross stitch (one stitch laid over another). Whichever method you choose, start from the wrong side of the felt piece on which you are working. All the patterns specify using an embroidery needle unless you are sewing on beads, in which case you should use a special beading needle. This has a very narrow head so that the beads slip over it easily.

If you aren't used to embroidering, practice the stitches a few times on a felt scrap before working on a zombie. None of the stitches described are difficult, but one or two—French knots in particular—can take some practice to get perfect.

THE STITCHES

OVERSTITCHING

Overstitching is used to attach two pieces of fabric together. This isn't a decorative stitch, so always use thread that matches the color of the felt, and keep the stitches small and neat.

1. Take a strand of embroidery floss and align the two pieces of fabric to be stitched together. Bring the thread through from the wrong side of one of the pieces and make a small stitch at right angles to the edges of both felt pieces, going over both edges and taking the needle through both layers of felt.

2. Push the needle back through the felt, bringing it out a little farther along from where you started, and make a second stitch over the edges of both pieces of felt.

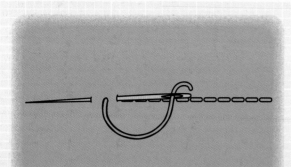

BACKSTITCH

This stitch makes a plain unbroken line.

1 Thread the needle with one or two strands of floss, as directed, then bring it up through the fabric at the point at which you want the line of stitching to start.

2 Make a stitch going in the opposite direction to the way you want your backstitch line to continue, and bring the needle back up through the fabric one stitch length away in the direction in which you want your stitching line to go.

3 Take the thread backward and push the needle through the point where the first stitch finished. Bring it out one stitch length in front of the thread. Continue until the length of the desired line of backstitch is complete. Fasten off.

SATIN STITCH

This stitch is useful for filling small areas solidly.

To cover small areas, make single, long parallel stitches alongside one another. This will make a solid area of threads.

Satin stitch is usually done neatly with stitches running exactly parallel. For the rather more grisly effects (clotted blood, for example!) called for in some of the zombies, make small areas of satin stitch a little more uneven—you can overlap stitches slightly, or set them at a small angle to one another. For really gruesome "clotting" when you're sewing bloodstains, try adding one or two French knots to areas of satin stitch.

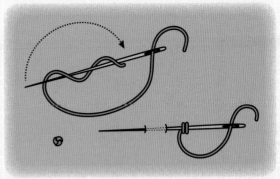

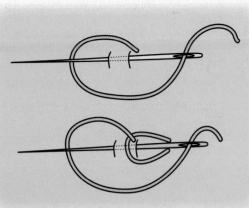

CHAIN STITCH

This stitch makes a decorative line of linked loops.

1. Bring your threaded needle up through the fabric, then bring the spare thread out in front of your needle and make a loop around it. Reinsert the needle in the fabric and bring it out again one stitch length in front of your first stitch and through the loop of thread.

2. Pull the thread tightly enough to make an oval-shaped stitch that lies flat. Repeat both steps to continue the chain of stitches.

FRENCH KNOT

This stitch makes a small decorative knot that stands above the surface of the felt.

1. Thread a needle with the number of strands specified in the instructions, fasten the end on the wrong side of the felt, and bring the needle out on the right side where you want to make your French knot. Use your left thumb to hold down the thread at the point at which it emerges from the felt, and wrap the thread twice around the needle.

2. Keep your thumb in place on the felt and bring the needle back through the felt very close to where it emerged (not in the exact same spot, though, or the thread will simply pull back through the hole).

3. Push the needle through to the back of the felt and pull the thread taut. A small textured knot will be left on the right side of the felt. Fasten off the thread on the wrong side, or go on to make your next French knot.

Double and triple French knots can be made when you want the finished knot to be larger. They're made by winding the thread two or three more times around the needle. You need to be very careful that the thread doesn't tangle when you're pulling it back through the felt.

BEADING

Use a beading needle to add beads and sequins. Beads are sewn on simply by bringing the needle through from the back of the felt, threading the bead onto the needle, then pushing the needle back through near where it first emerged and pulling the thread tight.

To add a sequin, bring the needle up through the felt, thread on the sequin, and secure it by taking a stitch over to the edge on each side (or use more stitches, to make a decorative star shape on top of your sequin). Alternatively, use a bead to secure the sequin in the center, as shown below right.

TO SECURE A SEQUIN WITH A BEAD

1 Thread a beading needle and bring it up through the felt to the right side. Thread first the sequin and then the bead onto the needle.

2 Take the needle back through the central hole of the sequin, pull the thread tight, and fasten off securely at the back of the felt. The bead, larger than the central hole of the sequin, will hold the sequin in place.

3 To add more beads, make a short stitch to the next point and add the next bead. Repeat and then fasten off securely at the back.

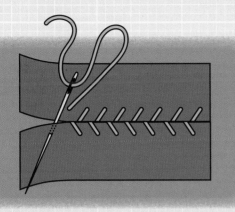

BASEBALL STITCH

Baseball stitch is used to join two edges that abut one another. The bodies of the zombie felties that are a cone or cylinder shape are closed up using this stitch.

1. Bring a needle up through one piece of fabric a little way in from the edge (the length that you want your stitch to be).

2. Take it down through the space between the two pieces of fabric that you are joining, and bring it up through the back of the other edge, a stitch's length in.

3. Repeat, going between the space and up through the other piece of fabric, to make a row of stitches that go alternately between the two pieces of fabric.

TIPS

* Pay attention to the difficulty levels, which are shown as skull ratings. The easiest zombies are marked with one skull, slightly harder ones with two, and so on. Don't attempt a three-skull zombie until you've tried a few at the simpler levels!

* Pick one of the darker-colored zombies for your first project—when you're starting out, you'll be more likely to handle the felt and the paler colors can become grubby as you work.

* Felt doesn't fray, so it's good for working at this scale, but when a piece or pieces are particularly tiny, you may find that it helps to scrape a very, very thin layer of craft glue over the wrong side of the fabric and allow it to dry before you cut them out. This makes the fabric slightly stiffer, and the cut pieces will have nice sharp edges.

CLASSIC ZOMBIE

Graying flesh dropping from exposed teeth? Check. Spiky wisps of hair sticking out all over? Check. Moldy bandages trailing around lurching limbs? Check. It's the classic zombie: the one that's graced a thousand B movies. Coming soon to a sewing table near you.

YOU WILL NEED

* 6-inch (15-cm) square of pale gray felt
* 4-inch (10-cm) square of dark gray felt
* 4-inch (10-cm) square of cream felt
* Small scrap of white felt
* Embroidery floss in black, white, red, pale gray, and dark gray
* 2 small black bugle beads
* 4 white bugle beads
* 1 black sequin
* 1 round white bead, about ¼ inch (6 mm) in diameter
* 1 round white bead, about ½ inch (1.25 cm) in diameter
* 2 tiny black beads
* 12-inch (30-cm) length of black necklace cord
* Tiny quantity of toy stuffing
* Embroidery needle
* Beading needle
* Scissors
* Pencil
* Tracing paper
* Craft glue
* Matchstick or tweezers to help with stuffing

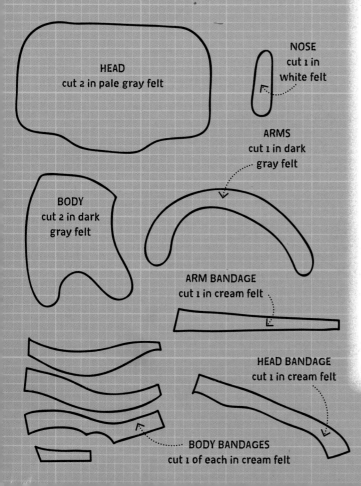

HEAD
cut 2 in pale gray felt

NOSE
cut 1 in white felt

ARMS
cut 1 in dark gray felt

BODY
cut 2 in dark gray felt

ARM BANDAGE
cut 1 in cream felt

HEAD BANDAGE
cut 1 in cream felt

BODY BANDAGES
cut 1 of each in cream felt

TO MAKE CLASSIC ZOMBIE

1 Cut out all the felt pieces as marked, either photocopying or scanning the templates, or using tracing paper to make templates as described on page 4. Stick the nose piece in place on one of the head pieces with craft glue. Thread a beading needle with 1 strand of black floss and stitch the black bugle beads in place on the nose piece.

2 Thread a beading needle with 1 strand of white floss and stitch the 4 white bugle beads in place under the nose to make teeth. Thread an embroidery needle with 6 strands of black floss and sew a large cross stitch where the zombie's left eye will dangle. Thread a beading needle with 2 strands of black floss and sew the right eye in place by taking the needle through the felt, then through the black sequin, the smaller of the 2 round white beads, and one of the tiny black beads, then back through the larger bead, the sequin, and the felt.

3 Add the dangling eyeball: Thread a beading needle with 2 strands of red floss and push it from the wrong side of the felt through the center of the cross stitch that makes the left eye. Feed first the second tiny black bead and then the larger round white bead onto it. Thread the needle back through the center of the white bead, then sew the floss back through the felt, leaving enough slack for the eyeball to dangle on the cheek. When the loop is the right length, bring the floss back through from the wrong side of the felt and wind more red floss around the loop of the eyeball to strengthen it. Finish off the floss on the wrong side of the felt.

Glue the bandage across the left-hand top of the head, taking the ends around to the back.

4 Cut the necklace cord into 10 even lengths and glue them in place on the inside of the second head piece. Thread an embroidery needle with 1 strand of pale gray floss, align the 2 head pieces, and sew them together with a small overstitch. Leave a gap at the base and pad the head lightly with wisps of stuffing, using a matchstick or tweezers to help you. Then stitch the gap closed.

5 Add the 4 body bandages to the front of one of the body pieces, gluing them in place and taking the ends around to the wrong side of the felt.

6 Glue the single arm unit to the wrong side of the second body piece, very slightly below the top edge. Wrap and glue the arm bandage twice around the right arm.

7 Thread an embroidery needle with 1 strand of dark gray floss, align the body pieces, and stitch them together using a small overstitch. Pass the needle to the side of the bandages so that the stitches don't show. Leave the neck open. Pad the body with wisps of stuffing, using a matchstick or tweezers to fill it evenly. Stitch the body closed.

8 Thread an embroidery needle with 2 strands of dark gray floss and stitch the body to the back of the head. Finally, trim the spikes of hair to make raggedly different lengths.

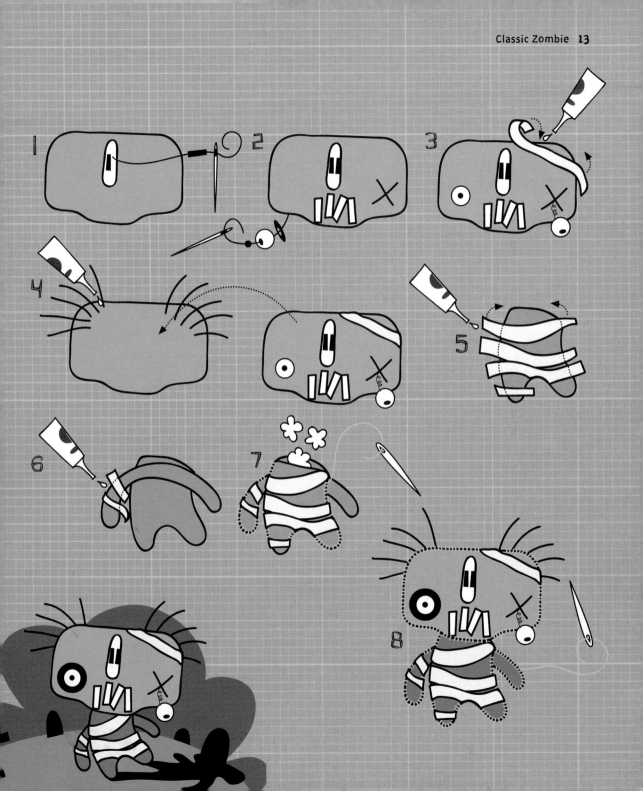

ZOMBIE PUPPY

You can tell that this pup didn't come out of any ordinary breeding program. You may be able to get over his gleaming red eyes and his cold, unpuppylike demeanor. But what's that he's chewing, with the clotted red stuff all over it? Could it be...?

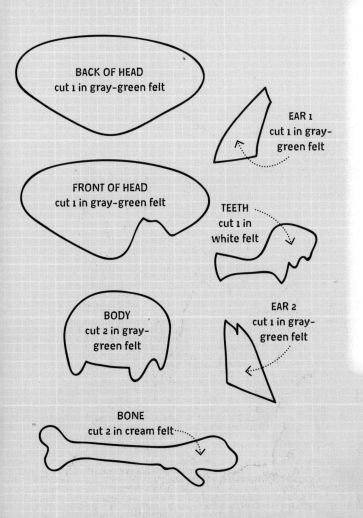

BACK OF HEAD
cut 1 in gray-green felt

EAR 1
cut 1 in gray-green felt

FRONT OF HEAD
cut 1 in gray-green felt

TEETH
cut 1 in white felt

BODY
cut 2 in gray-green felt

EAR 2
cut 1 in gray-green felt

BONE
cut 2 in cream felt

YOU WILL NEED

* 6-inch (15-cm) square of gray-green felt
* 2-inch (5-cm) square of white felt
* 2-inch (5-cm) square of cream felt
* Embroidery floss in pink, black, white, red, and gray-green
* 2 flat oval red beads, about ¼ inch (6 mm) long
* Tiny quantity of toy stuffing
* Embroidery needle
* Beading needle
* Scissors
* Pencil
* Tracing paper
* Craft glue
* Matchstick or tweezers to help with stuffing

TO MAKE ZOMBIE PUPPY

1 Cut out all the felt pieces as marked, either photocopying or scanning the templates, or using tracing paper to make templates as described on page 4. Stick the teeth in position on the back of the head front piece with craft glue. Check the photograph of the finished piece for placement.

2 Thread an embroidery needle with 2 strands of pink floss and use satin stitch to embroider a patch of pink "gums" at the top of the tooth piece.

3 Thread an embroidery needle with 2 strands of black floss and use satin stitch to make Puppy's nose, checking with the photograph to get the shape right. Rethread the needle with 2 strands of white floss and make the highlight on the nose with 2 or 3 smaller stitches. Then thread a beading needle with 2 strands of red floss and sew on the 2 red beads for Puppy's eyes.

4 Glue the ears in position on the back of Zombie Puppy's head, checking the photograph of the finished piece for placement.

5 Align the 2 felt head pieces and stitch them together using an embroidery needle threaded with 1 strand of gray-green floss and a small overstitch. Just catch the thread when sewing around the back of the teeth so that the stitches don't show. Leave a gap at the top of the head and stuff with wisps of toy stuffing, using a matchstick or tweezers to help you. Stitch the gap closed.

6 Glue the 2 felt body pieces together, then stitch the top of the body to the back of Zombie Puppy's head, using 1 strand of gray-green floss and a small overstitch. Make small individual stitches under the puppy's chin to hold it down against the body piece.

7 Align the 2 bone pieces and use a tiny quantity of craft glue to stick them together.

8 When the glue is dry, thread an embroidery needle with 2 strands of red floss and embroider the blood in satin stitch. If you'd like to, add a few French knots to look like clots and drips.

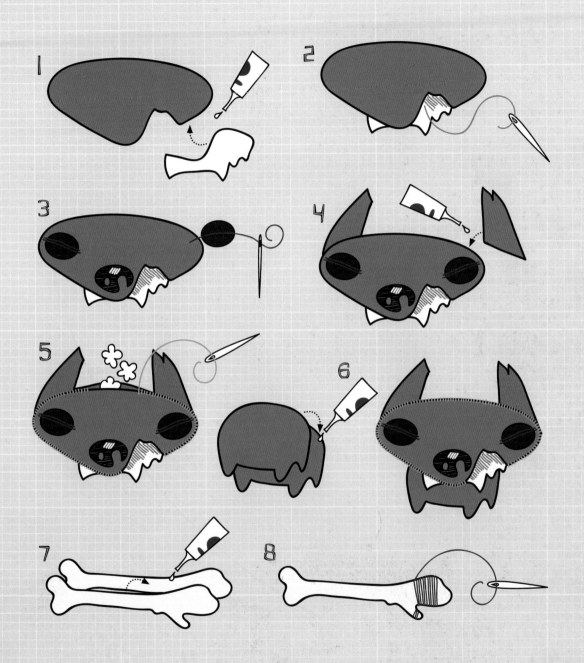

ZOMBIE KITTY

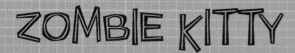

In life she finished off mice and other vermin; now that she's joined the zombies, she's ready and able to tackle bigger prey. This grim little feline has moved way beyond a saucer of milk: These days, she's pure carnivore.

YOU WILL NEED

* 6-inch (15-cm) square of pale green felt
* Small scraps of red and pink felt
* Embroidery floss in pink, pale green, black, and red
* 8-inch (20-cm) length of black necklace cord
* 1 small round white bead, about ¼ inch (6 mm) in diameter
* 1 tiny black bead
* Tiny quantity of toy stuffing
* Embroidery needle
* Beading needle
* Scissors
* Pencil
* Tracing paper
* Craft glue
* Matchstick or tweezers to help with stuffing

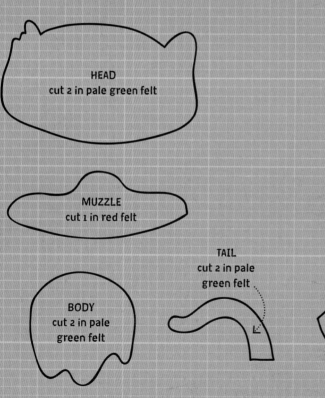

HEAD
cut 2 in pale green felt

MUZZLE
cut 1 in red felt

BODY
cut 2 in pale green felt

TAIL
cut 2 in pale green felt

COLLAR
cut 1 in pink felt

TO MAKE ZOMBIE KITTY

1 Cut out all the felt pieces as marked, either photocopying or scanning the templates, or using tracing paper to make templates as described on page 4. Use craft glue to stick the red muzzle piece in place on one of the head pieces.

2 Thread an embroidery needle with 2 strands of pink floss and stitch the nose, referring to the photograph for the positioning and making 3 straight, horizontal stitches on each side. Rethread the needle with 2 strands of pale green floss and sew the mouth using backstitch.

3 Thread a needle with 1 strand of black floss and stitch the eyes. Make each by backstitching a slanting row of 4 stitches, then make 4 uneven vertical stitches across the line, to make the eyes look as though they're sewn shut.

4 Cut the necklace cord into two 4-inch (10-cm) lengths. Fold them in half, thread a needle with 2 strands of pale green floss, and sew the cord onto the inner side of the second head piece for whiskers. (You can trim them to length later.)

5 Align the 2 tail pieces and stick them together with craft glue. Thread an embroidery needle with 2 strands of red floss and stitch the "blood" onto the end of the tail, using a large overstitch along each side of the tail tip. Stick the tail in position on the wrong side of the second head piece.

6 Thread an embroidery needle with 1 strand of pale green floss, align the 2 head pieces, and sew them together using a small overstitch. Leave a gap open under the chin, pad the head lightly with stuffing using a matchstick or tweezers to help you, then stitch the gap closed.

7 Stick the pink collar piece in position on one of the body pieces, then thread a beading needle with 1 strand of black floss and stitch the white and black beads onto the collar to give an eyeball effect. Align the 2 body pieces and stick them together with craft glue.

8 Stitch the body onto the back of the head using an embroidery needle threaded with 1 strand of pale green floss, and a small overstitch. Finally, trim the whiskers to the right length and bend them into shape with your fingers.

DEAD DUCKY

Ducky died a long time ago at the shooting range—you can see the bullet holes. Since then, he's passed into a different state of being altogether. And it's not one in which he's going to be welcome sharing anybody's bath.

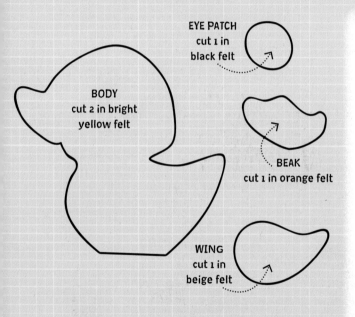

EYE PATCH
cut 1 in
black felt

BODY
cut 2 in bright
yellow felt

BEAK
cut 1 in orange felt

WING
cut 1 in
beige felt

YOU WILL NEED

* 6-inch (15-cm) square of bright yellow felt
* Small scraps of orange, beige, and black felt
* Embroidery floss in orange, white, red, and yellow
* 1 white sequin
* 3 tiny round black beads
* 6 white bugle beads
* Tiny quantity of toy stuffing
* Embroidery needle
* Beading needle
* Pair of pointed-nose pliers
* Scissors
* Pencil
* Tracing paper
* Craft glue
* Matchstick or tweezers to help with stuffing

TO MAKE DEAD DUCKY

1 Cut out all the felt pieces as marked, either photocopying or scanning the templates, or using tracing paper to make templates as described on page 4. Use craft glue to stick the beak, wing, and eye patch in place on one of the body pieces.

2 Thread an embroidery needle with 2 strands of orange floss and make the line around the lower edge and up the center of the beak with backstitch. Rethread the needle with 1 strand of white floss and stitch the sequin on in the center of the eye patch.

3 Thread an embroidery needle with 2 strands of red floss and make the four "bloodstained" areas with satin stitch, starting with the one around the eye patch and moving on to the smaller "bullet hole" areas, checking the photograph of the finished piece to place them correctly.

4 Thread a beading needle with 1 strand of red floss and stitch on the 3 tiny black beads to make the bullet holes, each at the top end of one of the embroidered bloodstains.

5 Thread an embroidery needle with 1 strand of yellow floss, align the 2 body pieces, and sew them together using a small overstitch. Overstitch through the layers of yellow felt around the beak, but catch the thread just under the glued-on beak piece so that the stitches don't show. Leave the base open.

6 Fill Ducky with small wisps of stuffing so that he is lightly padded all over. Use a matchstick or tweezers to help distribute the stuffing evenly. When the padding is in place, stitch the gap closed.

7 Using a pair of pointed-nose pliers, cut the white bugle beads until you have made 2 jagged "fangs." Put a cloth over your hand and the pliers, and cut carefully to avoid splinters of glass flying around. You may have to try 2 or 3 times before you get the right size and shape of pieces.

8 When you have 2 bead fangs of about the right size and length, thread a beading needle with 1 strand of white floss and stitch the teeth into place on Ducky's beak. Finish the thread neatly and hide the end inside Dead Ducky.

ZOMBIE BUNNY

DIFFICULTY RATING 💀💀

Surprisingly jolly given that he no longer boasts a pulse, Zombie Bunny can still hold a pose. Arms held high, dripping with gore, he charges forward. No rabbit hutch made by human hand can contain him. Are you *sure* he's your long-lost pet?

YOU WILL NEED

* 6-inch (15-cm) square of pea green felt
* Small scraps of cream and bright green felt
* Embroidery floss in black, pale pink, red, and pea green
* 1 black bead, about ¼ inch (6 mm) in diameter
* 1 shirt button with 4 holes, about ½ inch (1.25 cm) in diameter
* Tiny quantity of toy stuffing
* Embroidery needle
* Beading needle
* Scissors
* Pencil
* Tracing paper
* Craft glue
* Matchstick or tweezers to help with stuffing

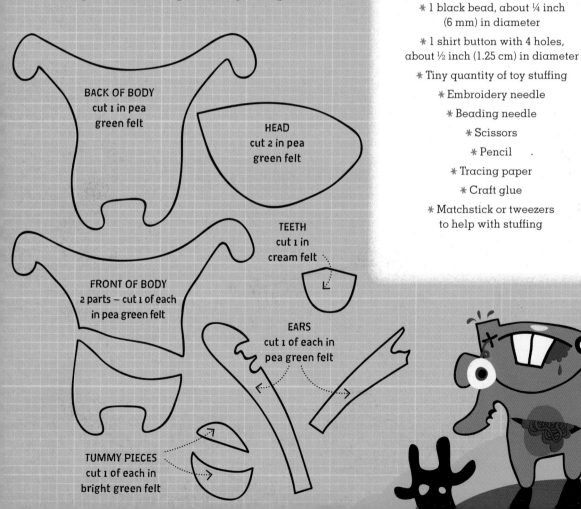

BACK OF BODY
cut 1 in pea green felt

HEAD
cut 2 in pea green felt

TEETH
cut 1 in cream felt

FRONT OF BODY
2 parts – cut 1 of each in pea green felt

EARS
cut 1 of each in pea green felt

TUMMY PIECES
cut 1 of each in bright green felt

TO MAKE ZOMBIE BUNNY

1 Cut out all the felt pieces as marked, either photocopying or scanning the templates, or using tracing paper to make templates as described on page 4. Use craft glue to stick the teeth to the front of one of the head pieces, checking the photograph to position the shape correctly. Thread an embroidery needle with 1 strand of black floss and make the topline of the mouth, above the teeth, with backstitch. Stitch the details of the teeth with running stitch.

2 Thread an embroidery needle with 2 strands of pale pink floss and make the nose with 4 satin stitches of decreasing size, creating a triangular shape. Thread a beading needle with 2 strands of black floss, sew a large cross stitch in position for the right eye, and sew on the black bead to make Bunny's left eye. Thread an embroidery needle with 3 strands of red floss and stitch on the button at the center of the cross stitch, leaving a loop of red thread, allowing the eyeball to dangle. Finally, sew the dripping blood at the corner of the mouth using 3 strands of red floss and giving it some bulk with a mixture of satin stitch and French knots.

3 Using craft glue, stick Zombie Bunny's ears in place on the back of the head piece.

4 Thread an embroidery needle with 1 strand of pea green floss, align the 2 head pieces, and sew them together using a small overstitch. Leave a gap at the top of the head, between the ears, pad the head with wisps of stuffing using a matchstick or tweezers to help you, then stitch the gap closed.

5 Thread an embroidery needle with 1 strand of pea green floss, align the 2 front body pieces with the single back piece, and sew around the edges using a small overstitch. Glue the bright green stomach patches in place on either side of the belly slit, then lightly pad the body with tiny wisps of toy stuffing, using a matchstick or tweezers to push them through the slit.

6 Unroll a few inches of red embroidery floss and wind them into a loose bundle about an inch (2.5 cm) long. Tie the bundle around the middle with a short length of floss. Place a dab of craft glue through the slit in the belly and stuff the floss bundle in loosely, leaving loops protruding to make Bunny's "guts."

7 Thread an embroidery needle with 1 strand of pea green floss and stitch the top of Bunny's body to the back of his head, using a small overstitch and taking it through only one layer of the head's felt. As you sew, fold the ears down behind Bunny's head and sew them in place with 1 or 2 holding stitches.

8 Finally, add the dripping blood to Bunny's paw. Thread an embroidery needle with 6 strands of red floss and sew around his left paw, looping the floss and adding 1 or 2 French knots to make the blood look thick and clotted.

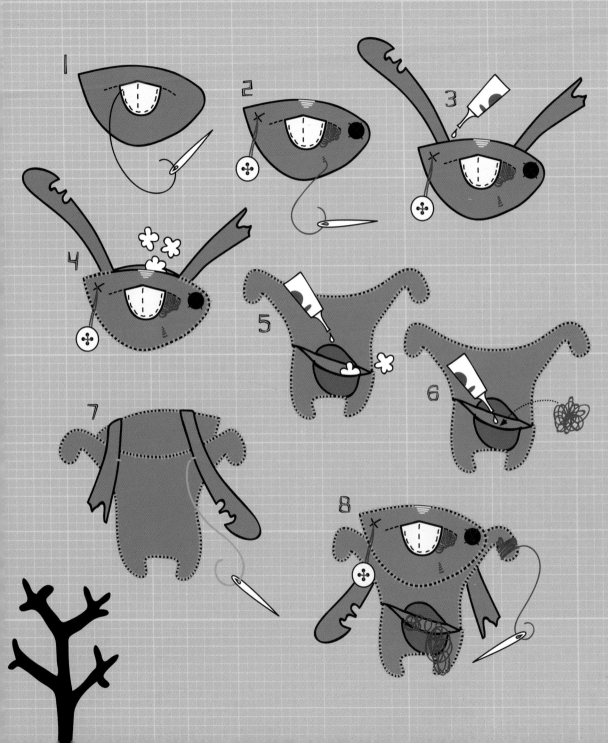

PUMPKIN HEAD

DIFFICULTY RATING

Mouth open in a silent yell, Pumpkin Head is just about as intimidating as a squash-based zombie could be. He's big, he's bad, and he's unquestionably king of his own hellish corner of the vegetable patch.

HEAD
cut 2 in bright orange felt

Cut the gray lines on front piece only

MOUTH
cut 1 in black felt

ARMS
cut 2 in pale gray felt

BODY
cut 2 in turquoise felt

BANDAGES
cut 1 of each in pale gray felt

YOU WILL NEED

* 4-inch (10-cm) square of bright orange felt
* 2-inch (5-cm) square of turquoise felt
* 2-inch (5-cm) square of pale gray felt
* Small scrap of black felt
* Embroidery floss in cream, dark orange, black, white, pink, bright orange, turquoise, and gray
* 2 tiny white beads
* 9 pink sequins
* Tiny quantity of toy stuffing
* Embroidery needle
* Beading needle
* Scissors
* Pencil
* Tracing paper
* Craft glue
* Matchstick or tweezers to help with stuffing

TO MAKE PUMPKIN HEAD

1 Cut out all the felt pieces as marked, either photocopying or scanning the templates, or using tracing paper to make templates as described on page 4. Take one of the head pieces and, using the points of a pair of sharp scissors, cut out the mouth cavity and make a slit where marked on the right-hand side of the head, as shown on the pattern. Use craft glue to stick the mouth behind the cavity, on the back of the head piece.

2 Thread an embroidery needle with 2 strands of cream floss and sew large, uneven stitches around the edge of the mouth, checking the photograph for placement. Rethread the needle with 2 strands of dark orange floss and sew 4 lines of running stitch on the head, following the positioning shown in the photograph.

3 Thread an embroidery needle with 2 strands of black floss and stitch 2 small ovals of satin stitch to make Pumpkin Head's eyes. Thread a beading needle with 1 strand of white floss and stitch a tiny white bead in the center of each eye.

4 Add the sequins for Pumpkin Head's brain. Thread a beading needle with 1 strand of pink floss and stitch the sequins on, working from the outer edge inward, overlapping sequins as you go. When all the sequins have been added, run a thin line of craft glue along the inside of the upper edge of the slit and glue down to secure.

5 Thread an embroidery needle with 1 strand of bright orange floss, align the 2 head pieces, and stitch them together. Start stitching just before the point at which the face is slit and pull the slit together with a stitch at the top, then carry on overstitching under the sequins. Leave a gap at the top of the head and pad it evenly with wisps of stuffing, using a matchstick or tweezers to help you. Stitch the gap closed.

6 Glue the gray "bandage" stripes onto one of the body pieces, wrapping them around the body and gluing the ends down at the back. Thread an embroidery needle with 3 strands of black floss and sew a line of backstitch vertically down the body, then make 6 single, uneven stitches at right angles to the line.

7 Align the 2 body pieces. Thread an embroidery needle with 1 strand of turquoise floss and sew them together with a small overstitch. Leave a gap at the neck, pad evenly with wisps of stuffing, as with the head, then stitch closed.

8 Thread an embroidery needle with 2 strands of gray floss and stitch the left arm in position at the back of the body and the right arm to the front, using 3 small stitches to secure each. Rethread the needle with 2 strands of turquoise floss and stitch the top of the body to the back of the head, checking the photograph to get the right angle.

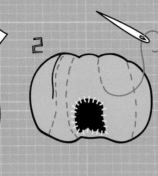

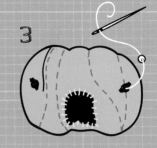

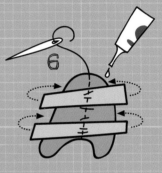

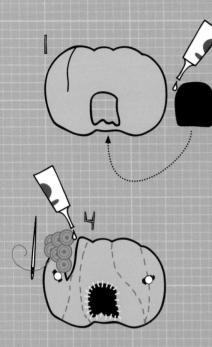

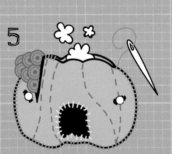

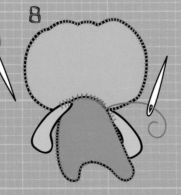

DAY OF THE DEAD

DIFFICULTY RATING

Pastel colors can't conceal her skeletal frame, nor a festive diadem disguise her vacant stare and her bony little nostrils—but this cute Dia de los Muertos celebrant still has a spring in her step. Even if her bones do rattle with every movement.

YOU WILL NEED

* 4-inch (10-cm) square of cream felt
* 2-inch (5-cm) square of turquoise felt
* Small scraps of white and yellow felt
* Fine metallic silver embroidery floss
* Embroidery floss in red, cream, yellow, green, and turquoise
* 10 tiny metallic green beads
* 1 yellow flower-shaped button, about ½ inch (1.25 cm) in diameter
* 1 large purple star- or flower-shaped sequin
* 1 green sequin
* 6 white bugle beads
* 1 red heart-shaped sequin
* Tiny quantity of toy stuffing
* Embroidery needle
* Beading needle
* Scissors
* Pencil
* Tracing paper
* Craft glue
* Matchstick or tweezers to help with stuffing

HEAD
cut 2 in cream felt

DIADEM 1
cut 1 in yellow felt

BODY
cut 2 in turquoise felt

DIADEM 2
cut 2 in yellow felt

BACKBONE
cut 1 in white felt

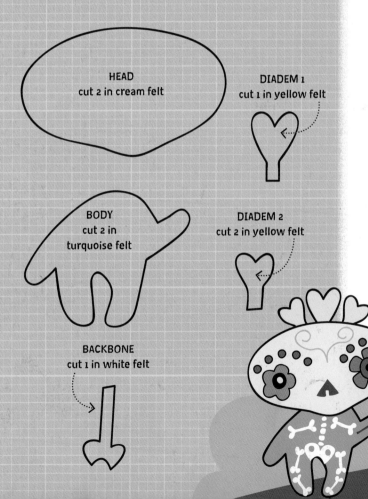

TO MAKE DAY OF THE DEAD

1 Cut out all the felt pieces as marked, except for the diadem pieces, either photocopying or scanning the templates, or using tracing paper to make templates as described on page 4. Trace around the diadem pieces on the felt and set them aside. Thread an embroidery needle with 1 strand of metallic silver floss and embroider the forehead swirl in backstitch on one of the head pieces. Rethread the needle with 2 strands of red floss and make the nose in an inverted heart shape with small satin stitches. Thread a beading needle with 1 strand of cream floss and stitch on 5 tiny metallic green beads in an arch for each eyebrow.

2 Using an embroidery needle and 2 strands of yellow floss, stitch the yellow button in place to make the right eye. Thread a beading needle with 2 strands of green floss and thread on first the purple, and then the green sequin. Stitch in place to make the left eye.

3 Because the pieces for the diadem are so small, it's easier to embroider them before cutting them out. Thread an embroidery needle with 2 strands of turquoise floss and embroider heart shapes on the diadem pieces in satin stitch. When the embroidery is completed, cut out the 3 shapes.

4 Use craft glue to stick the 3 diadem pieces in position on the wrong side of the front head piece. Leave to dry, then align the 2 head pieces, thread an embroidery needle with 1 strand of cream floss, and sew the head together using a small overstitch. Leave a gap at the base, pad lightly with wisps of stuffing, using a matchstick or tweezers to help you, then stitch closed.

5 Stick the white spine onto one of the body pieces with craft glue.

6 Thread a beading needle with 1 strand of turquoise floss and stitch the 6 bugle beads in place to make the rest of the "skeleton," referring to the photograph for placement.

7 Align the 2 body pieces and sew them together, using an embroidery needle threaded with 1 strand of turquoise floss and a small overstitch. Leave the neck open, pad lightly with wisps of stuffing, as with the head, then stitch closed.

8 Using an embroidery needle and 1 strand of turquoise floss, stitch the body to the back of the head, checking the photograph for positioning. Finally, thread a beading needle with 2 strands of red floss and stitch the heart sequin at the end of the left arm. Stitch down the arm in backstitch to create a "vein," and finish off neatly.

ZOMBIE SURFER

Even dudes can turn undead. Nothing, but nothing, is going to stop this little horror from cresting the waves. With his empty eyes and garish green shorts he's in the vanguard of cool zombie fashion—and he's accessorized with a particularly grisly surfboard.

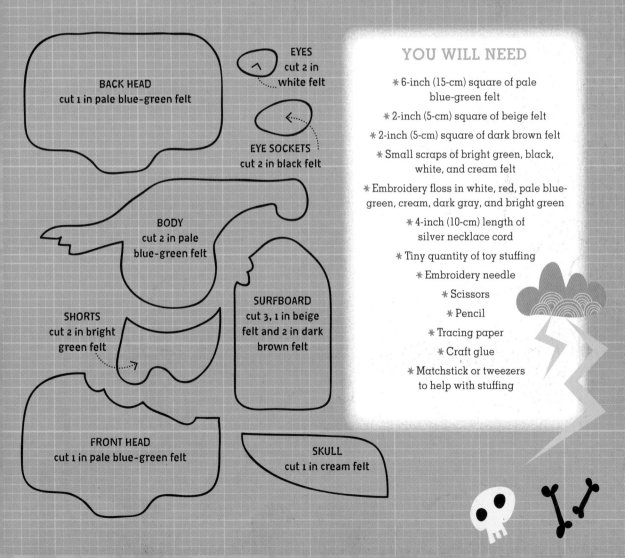

BACK HEAD
cut 1 in pale blue-green felt

EYES
cut 2 in white felt

EYE SOCKETS
cut 2 in black felt

BODY
cut 2 in pale blue-green felt

SHORTS
cut 2 in bright green felt

SURFBOARD
cut 3, 1 in beige felt and 2 in dark brown felt

FRONT HEAD
cut 1 in pale blue-green felt

SKULL
cut 1 in cream felt

YOU WILL NEED

* 6-inch (15-cm) square of pale blue-green felt
* 2-inch (5-cm) square of beige felt
* 2-inch (5-cm) square of dark brown felt
* Small scraps of bright green, black, white, and cream felt
* Embroidery floss in white, red, pale blue-green, cream, dark gray, and bright green
* 4-inch (10-cm) length of silver necklace cord
* Tiny quantity of toy stuffing
* Embroidery needle
* Scissors
* Pencil
* Tracing paper
* Craft glue
* Matchstick or tweezers to help with stuffing

TO MAKE ZOMBIE SURFER

1 Cut out all the felt pieces as marked, either photocopying or scanning the templates, or using tracing paper to make templates as described on page 4. Stick the skull piece in place on the back of the front head. Thread an embroidery needle with 2 strands of white floss and make a row of uneven stitches at right angles to join.

2 Use craft glue to stick on the eye socket pieces, then stick a white eye piece in the center of each. Thread an embroidery needle with 2 strands of red floss and make the nose with satin stitch.

3 Cut 4 short, uneven lengths from the piece of necklace cord and use craft glue to stick them in place on the lower edge of the back head piece. Then align the head pieces, thread an embroidery needle with 1 strand of pale blue-green floss, and stitch them together using a small overstitch, sewing carefully between the protruding "beard" pieces of necklace cord. Leave the exposed skull section open. Pad the head with wisps of stuffing, using a matchstick or tweezers to help you distribute it evenly. Then rethread the embroidery needle with 1 strand of cream floss and stitch the gap closed.

4 Glue the green felt shorts pieces onto the body pieces, front and back. Thread an embroidery needle with 1 strand of dark gray floss and make small backstitch lines for the ribs on one of the body pieces, 3 on each side, checking the photograph of the finished Surfer for placement.

5 Align the 2 body pieces and glue the 2 ends of the right arm together with craft glue. Thread an embroidery needle with 1 strand of bright green floss and stitch the green portion of the body pieces together with a small overstitch. Rethread the needle with 1 strand of pale blue-green floss and overstitch around the rest of the body, leaving a gap open at the neck. Pad the body with wisps of stuffing, as for the head, then stitch the gap closed. Make a tiny knotted loop "bow" with 2 strands of white floss and stitch it in place on the front of Zombie Surfer's shorts.

6 Rethread the needle with 1 strand of pale blue-green floss and use a small overstitch to sew the body onto the back of the head, checking the photograph of the finished piece for the degree of overlap.

7 Now make Zombie Surfer's gravestone surfboard. Thread an embroidery needle with 1 strand of white floss and make a line of running stitch around the beige felt gravestone piece. Rethread the needle with 2 strands of dark gray floss and stitch a minute skull and crossbones shape at top center. The crossbones are long single stitches with satin stitch ends; the skull is a backstitch skull-shaped outline with French knots for eye sockets.

8 Align all 3 gravestone pieces and then use craft glue to stick them together, with the beige layer uppermost.

BABY ZOMBIE

DIFFICULTY RATING
☠ ☠ ☠

From the grave to the cradle. You might fear that Baby Zombie would choke on the lollipop clutched in his tiny fist, but his grim little mouth is already stopped with a pacifier, and there's spooky green stuff trickling down his chin. Baby Zombie's lollipop is *extremely* sharp and he should be kept out of the reach of children.

YOU WILL NEED

* 4-inch (10-cm) square of pale green felt
* 6-inch (15-cm) square of gray-blue felt
* Small scrap of dirty pink felt
* 2-inch (5-cm) length of translucent green ribbon
* Embroidery floss in dirty pink, pale green, dark gray, gray-blue, and white
* 1 small gold ring-shaped jewelry finding, about ¼ inch (6 mm) in diameter
* 1 small round pearl bead
* 2 small round red beads
* 1 white bugle bead
* 1 flat circular multicolored glass bead, about ¼ inch (6 mm) in diameter
* 1 small embroidery needle (to make the lolly stick), about 1½ inches (4 cm) long
* Tiny quantity of toy stuffing
* Embroidery needle
* Beading needle
* Scissors
* Pencil
* Tracing paper
* Fast-drying epoxy glue
* Craft glue
* Matchstick or tweezers to help with stuffing

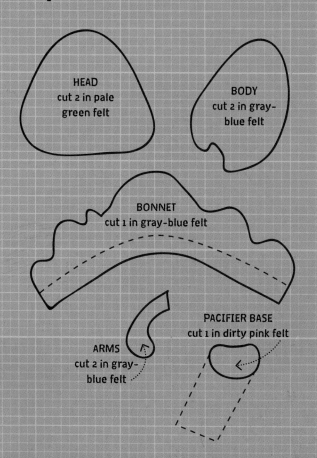

HEAD
cut 2 in pale green felt

BODY
cut 2 in gray-blue felt

BONNET
cut 1 in gray-blue felt

ARMS
cut 2 in gray-blue felt

PACIFIER BASE
cut 1 in dirty pink felt

TO MAKE BABY ZOMBIE

1 Cut out all the felt pieces as marked, either photocopying or scanning the templates, or using tracing paper to make templates as described on page 4. Cut 2 pieces of drool, following the dotted line around the pacifier template shape, from the translucent green ribbon. Trim the shapes so that they fit neatly behind the pacifier base at the top.

2 Stick the double layer of ribbon in place on one of the head pieces, then stick the pacifier base over the top part with craft glue. Thread an embroidery needle with 1 strand of dirty pink floss and sew a small overstitch around the pacifier piece. Use sharp scissors to shred the loose end of the ribbon slightly.

3 Open the gold ring, then close it through the hole in the pearl bead. Thread a beading needle with 1 strand of dirty pink floss and stitch the bead and ring in place at the center of the pacifier base on the face.

4 Thread a beading needle with 1 strand of pale green floss and stitch the red beads in place on the face to make the eyes. Thread an embroidery needle with 2 strands of dark gray floss and use backstitch to sew the curl on the forehead.

5 Thread an embroidery needle with 2 strands of gray-blue floss and make a line of running stitch along the stitch line on the bonnet. Pull the thread up so that the bonnet gathers slightly, and place it around the face, adjusting it until it fits.

When you've arranged the gathers evenly, knot the thread. Sandwich the bonnet between the head pieces, thread an embroidery needle with 1 strand of pale green floss, and sew together with a small overstitch, going through all 3 layers. Leave a gap at the base and pad the head with wisps of toy stuffing, using a matchstick or tweezers to distribute it evenly. Stitch the head closed.

6 Glue the arms in place on the inside of one of the body pieces. Thread an embroidery needle with 2 strands of dark gray floss and embroider a line of backstitch on the front of the second body piece, then make uneven single stitches at angles across it. Make 2 French knots in position for the eyes of the skull motif, then rethread the needle with 2 strands of white floss and sew the rest of the skull shape with satin stitch.

7 Align the 2 body pieces. Thread an embroidery needle with 1 strand of gray-blue floss and stitch them together with a small overstitch, leaving a gap at the neck. Stuff the body, as the head, then stitch it closed. Stitch the body onto the back of the head, checking with the photograph to get the angle between the head and neck right.

8 To make the lollipop, add a tiny drop of epoxy glue to the end of the embroidery needle that is to form the stick, then quickly thread on the white bugle bead and the circular bead. When the glue is dry, push the needle through Baby Zombie's "hand" and into his body, and glue it in place.

ZOMBIE UNDERTAKER

DIFFICULTY RATING

To get undead, you have to die first. And who better to manage the interment than an undead mortician, brain exposed and alive with pearly little maggots? Grave in demeanor, grim in appearance, and perfect for the role, he's even brought a suitable coffin to manage the occasion (see pages 78–79).

YOU WILL NEED

* 4-inch (10-cm) square of beige felt
* 4-inch (10-cm) square of black felt
* Embroidery floss in pink, black, white, and beige
* 12 pink sequins
* 8 tiny pearl beads
* 8 small pearl beads
* 8 white bugle beads
* Tiny quantity of toy stuffing
* Embroidery needle
* Beading needle
* Scissors
* Pencil
* Tracing paper
* Craft glue
* Matchstick or tweezers to help with stuffing

BODY
cut 2 in black felt

HANDS
cut 2 in beige felt

HAT
cut 2 in black felt

BACK OF HEAD
cut 1 in beige felt

FOREHEAD
cut 1 in beige felt

FRONT OF HEAD
cut 1 in beige felt

HAT BAND
cut 2 in black felt

EYE SOCKETS
cut 2 in black felt

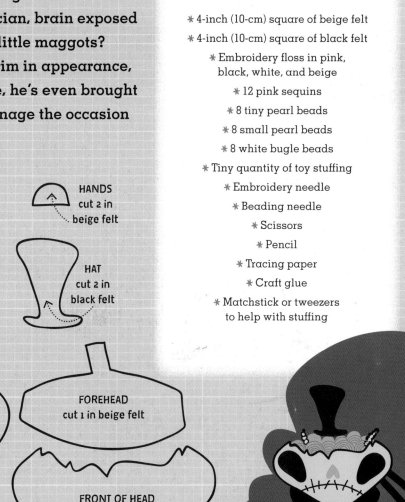

TO MAKE ZOMBIE UNDERTAKER

1 Cut out all the felt pieces as marked, either photocopying or scannng the templates, or using tracing paper to make templates as described on page 4. Stick the eye sockets on the front head piece with craft glue. Thread an embroidery needle with 2 strands of pink floss and make the nose with small, overlapping satin stitches. Rethread the needle with 1 strand of black floss and make the mouth with a line of backstitch, referring to the photograph to place it correctly. Cross the mouth with 8 single, slightly angled and uneven stitches.

2 Thread a beading needle with 1 strand of pink floss, and stitch the sequins onto the forehead piece, starting by overlapping them slightly over the top edge and working inward, continuing to overlap them as you work down. Leave the "stem" clear of sequins; it will be used as the base on which to glue the top hat.

3 Add the maggots—each is made from 4 pearl beads in 2 sizes, a smaller one at each end of a pair of larger ones. Thread a beading needle with 1 strand of white floss and thread it through the felt and the sequins where you want to add a maggot, then thread on first a tiny bead, then 2 larger ones, then one more tiny one. Bring the thread around the end bead and take it back through the other 3, then stitch it back through the felt, pulling tightly to hold the maggot in a line. Repeat 3 times, checking with the photograph for placement.

4 Use craft glue to stick the hat pieces on either side of the forehead "stem," aligning them carefully with each other. Then align the forehead with the front head piece to make a whole face and glue the 2 pieces together.

5 Stick the 2 hat bands on the inside of the back head piece, then align the front and back heads and sew them together using an embroidery needle threaded with 1 strand of beige embroidery floss and a small overstitch. Sew the felt edges just behind the sequins at the top of the head. Leave a gap at the base of the head and pad with wisps of stuffing, using a matchstick or tweezers to help you. Stitch the gap closed.

6 Glue the hands in place on the front of one of the body pieces. Thread a beading needle with 1 strand of beige embroidery floss and sew 4 bugle beads onto each hand to make bony fingers.

7 Align the 2 body pieces, thread an embroidery needle with 1 strand of black floss, and sew them together using a small overstitch. Leave a gap at the neck, pad with wisps of stuffing as with the head, then stitch the gap closed.

8 Stitch the body onto the back of the head, using overstitch and 1 strand of black floss. Check the photograph of the finished Zombie Undertaker to ensure that you get the right overlap of the body with the head.

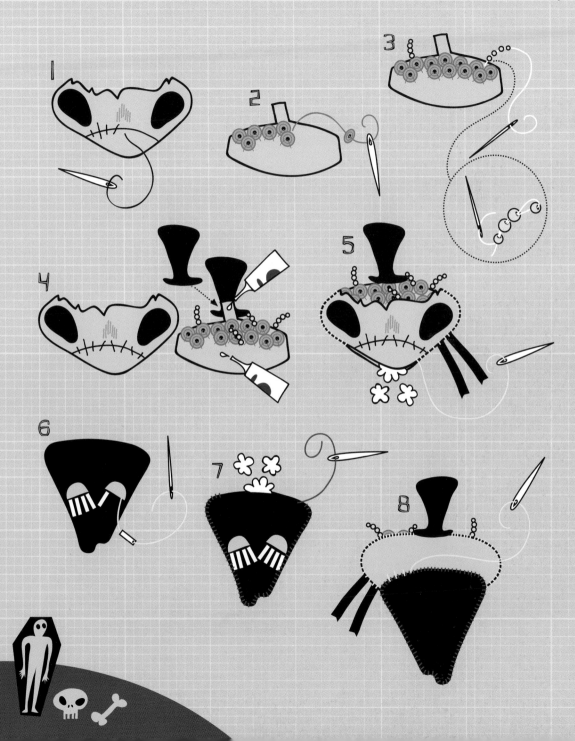

VAMPIRE ZOMBIE

What's that you say? Vampires and zombies don't mix? Ah, but sometimes they do. It's hard to say whether the nasty result is dead or undead, but despite the monocle and the suave presentation, this little creature is certainly rotten to the core...with fangs.

YOU WILL NEED

* 6-inch (15-cm) square of black felt
* 3-inch (7.5-cm) square of pale gray felt
* 2-inch (5-cm) square of green-gray felt
* Small scraps of white and red felt
* Embroidery floss in pink, red, black, pale gray, and pale yellow
* 1 silver ring-shaped jewelry finding, about ⅜ inch (1 cm) in diameter
* 1 tiny metallic bead
* 1 red glass bead about ¼ inch (6 mm) in diameter
* 2 round metallic sequins, one slightly larger than the other
* 4-inch (10-cm) length of silver necklace cord
* Tiny quantity of toy stuffing
* Embroidery needle
* Beading needle
* Tapestry needle
* Scissors
* Pencil
* Tracing paper
* Craft glue
* Matchstick or tweezers to help with stuffing

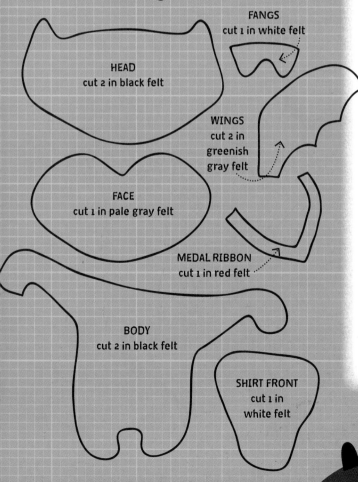

FANGS cut 1 in white felt

HEAD cut 2 in black felt

WINGS cut 2 in greenish gray felt

FACE cut 1 in pale gray felt

MEDAL RIBBON cut 1 in red felt

BODY cut 2 in black felt

SHIRT FRONT cut 1 in white felt

TO MAKE VAMPIRE ZOMBIE

1 Cut out all the felt pieces as marked, either photocopying or scanning the templates, or using tracing paper to make templates as described on page 4. Stick the face onto one of the head pieces, then stick the fangs in place with craft glue. Thread an embroidery needle with 2 strands of pink floss and embroider the nose in satin stitch, making a small heart shape. Rethread the needle with 4 strands of red floss and make the right eye with a large cross stitch. Rethread again with 2 strands of black floss and embroider the mouth shape around the fangs, using satin stitch.

2 Thread a beading needle with 2 strands of pale gray floss. Take the silver ring and loop one end of the necklace cord around its edge. Hold one end of the floss over the looped ends and wind the floss around the 2 pieces until they are firmly held together. Tie a knot around the wound floss, but don't cut the thread. Thread the tiny metallic bead onto the needle and sew the monocle onto the face, using the tiny bead to hold the rim of the monocle slightly clear of the face, then fasten off the floss at the back of the head piece.

3 Rethread the beading needle with 2 strands of red floss and sew the red bead onto the face, in the center of the monocle ring. Run a stitch through the bead and around the edge of the monocle ring to hold the monocle in place.

4 Align the head pieces. Thread an embroidery needle with 1 strand of black floss and stitch the head together using a small overstitch. Where the gray felt piece meets the black head piece, leave a gap, and pad the head slightly with wisps of toy stuffing, using a matchstick or tweezers to help you distribute it evenly. Rethread the needle with 1 strand of pale gray floss and stitch the head closed.

5 Glue the white shirt front in place on the front of one of the body pieces, then glue the red medal ribbon on top of the shirt front. Thread a beading needle with 1 strand of pale yellow floss and thread on first the large and then the smaller sequin. Use a couple of stitches to hold them in place at the lowest part of the medal ribbon.

6 Use craft glue to stick the wings in place on the inner side of the second body piece.

7 Align the body pieces with the wings sandwiched between them. Thread an embroidery needle with 1 strand of black floss and sew the pieces together using a small overstitch. Leave a gap open at the neck and stuff the body, as the head. When the stuffing is even, stitch the body closed. Stitch the body onto the back of the head with overstitch, using the same needle and floss.

8 Make a small hole in Vampire Zombie's left wing with the tapestry needle, and feed the loose end of the monocle's cord through it. Trim the end so that it fits neatly on the back of the body, and stitch it firmly in place using an embroidery needle and 2 strands of black floss.

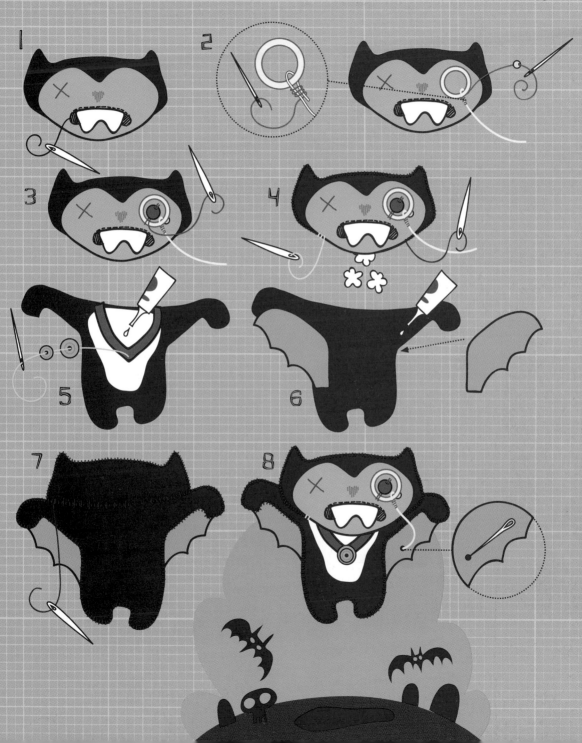

THRILLA

DIFFICULTY RATING

Still full of innate and deadly style, the original pop zombie has lost none of his mojo. He's gyrating wildly to a tune that only he can hear—nothing can stop him, and nobody sane would even try...

YOU WILL NEED

* 6-inch (15-cm) square of very pale green felt
* 4-inch (10-cm) square of red felt
* 4-inch (10-cm) square of black felt
* Small scrap of white felt
* Embroidery floss in black, pale green, pink, very pale green, and red
* 2 small red glass beads
* 8 pink sequins
* 4-inch (10-cm) length of black necklace cord
* Tiny quantity of toy stuffing
* Embroidery needle
* Beading needle
* Scissors
* Pencil
* Tracing paper
* Craft glue
* Matchstick or tweezers to help with stuffing

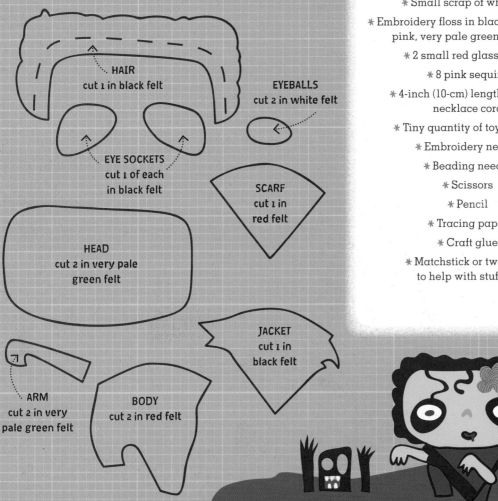

HAIR
cut 1 in black felt

EYEBALLS
cut 2 in white felt

EYE SOCKETS
cut 1 of each in black felt

SCARF
cut 1 in red felt

HEAD
cut 2 in very pale green felt

JACKET
cut 1 in black felt

ARM
cut 2 in very pale green felt

BODY
cut 2 in red felt

TO MAKE THRILLA

1 Cut out all the felt pieces as marked, either photocopying or scanning the templates, or using tracing paper to make templates as described on page 4. Stick the eye sockets and eyeballs in place on one of the head pieces with craft glue, checking the photograph for the correct placement. Thread a beading needle with 1 strand of black floss and sew a red bead in the center of each eyeball to make the pupils.

2 Thread an embroidery needle with 2 strands of pale green floss and make Thrilla's nose with 2 stitches on each side in an inverted "V" shape. Rethread the needle with 2 strands of black floss and make the mouth with 4 straight stitches in the shape of a rectangle.

3 Cut the necklace cord into 2 pieces and sew them in place on the forehead in loose curves, following the shape in the photograph and leaving long ends at the edge of the face. Use an embroidery needle threaded with 1 strand of black floss to sew the cord down with small single stitches across its width. Thread a beading needle with 1 strand of pink floss and stitch the sequins on to make the "brain." Start from the outer edge of the head and overlap them as you sew.

4 Align the face pieces together, sandwiching the hair between them and tucking the loose ends of necklace cord inside. Thread an embroidery needle with 1 strand of very pale green floss and sew the head together using a small overstitch, sewing through the hair as you go. Leave a gap open at the base, pad the head lightly with wisps of stuffing using a matchstick or tweezers to help you, then sew the gap closed.

5 Use craft glue to stick Thrilla's right arm in place on one of the body pieces. Stick the jacket in position on top of it (check with a photograph of the finished piece for placement), then add the red scarf. Thread an embroidery needle with 1 strand of black floss and make a line in running stitch around the scarf's border.

6 Thread an embroidery needle with 1 strand of the very pale green floss and stitch the left arm to the front of the body. Rethread the needle with 1 strand of red floss, align the 2 body pieces, and sew them together with a small overstitch. Leave a gap open at the neck, and pad with wisps of stuffing, as with the head.

7 Stitch the top of the body closed through all the felt layers.

8 Use 1 strand of red floss to stitch the body to the back of the head, following the photograph of Thrilla to get the angle right.

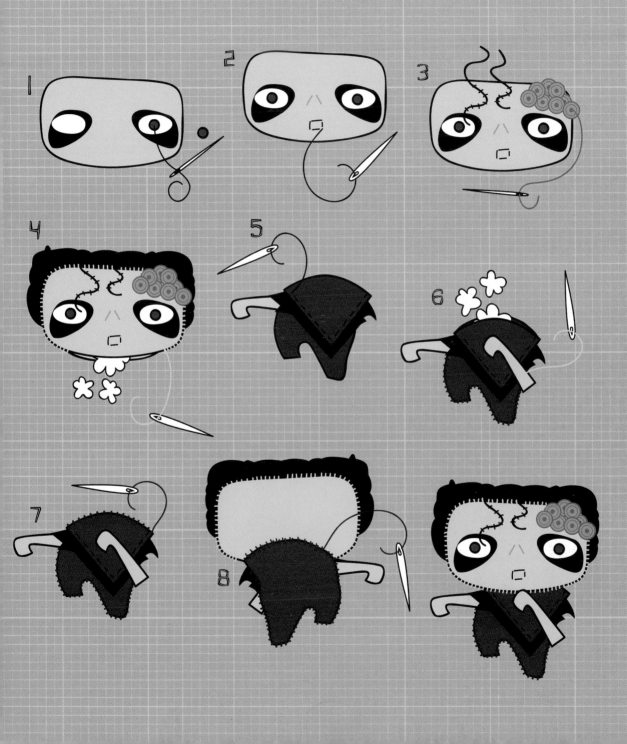

PIRATE ZOMBIE

DIFFICULTY RATING 💀 💀 💀

Bad things can happen on the high seas and this little shocker is no Captain Jack Sparrow. Hook, hollow eye sockets, and a rattling leg made of bones all add up to someone (or something) that you'd cheerfully walk the plank to avoid.

HAT
cut 1 in black felt

ARM
cut 1 in black felt

BODY
cut 2 in black felt

HEAD
cut 2 in light gray felt

SHIRT FRONT
cut 1 in white felt

EYE
cut 1 in black felt

EYE PATCH
cut 1 in black felt

MOUTH
cut 1 in black felt

YOU WILL NEED

* 4-inch (10-cm) square of black felt
* 4-inch (10-cm) square of pale gray felt
* Small scraps of white and black felt
* Embroidery floss in black, white, red, and pale gray
* 1 small faceted red glass bead, about ¼ inch (6 mm) long
* 4 tiny white beads
* 2 tiny silver beads
* 2 white bugle beads
* 1 small metal hook (taken from a hook-and-ring jewelry finding)
* 12-inch (30-cm) length of black necklace cord
* Tiny quantity of toy stuffing
* Embroidery needle
* Beading needle
* Scissors
* Pencil
* Tracing paper
* Craft glue
* Matchstick or tweezers to help with stuffing

TO MAKE PIRATE ZOMBIE

1 Cut out all the felt pieces as marked, either photocopying or scanning the templates, or using tracing paper to make templates as described on page 4. Use craft glue to stick the eye patch, eye, and mouth onto the front of one of the head pieces.

2 Stitch the face details. Thread an embroidery needle with 2 strands of black floss and make the eye patch string with backstitch. Rethread the needle with 2 strands of white floss and make single irregular stitches around the mouth, following the photograph for placement. Finally, thread a beading needle with 2 strands of red floss and stitch on the red glass bead to make the left eye.

3 Thread a beading needle with 1 strand of pale gray thread and make a running stitch line around the edge of the hat, then stitch on 2 of the tiny white beads at the top front. Glue the hat in place on the wrong side of the second head piece. Cut the necklace cord into 6 even lengths and glue them in place on the same side of the second head piece as the hat, 3 on each side.

4 Align the head pieces and sew them together with 1 strand of pale gray floss, using a small overstitch. Leave a gap at the base and stuff the head lightly before stitching closed.

5 Glue the white shirt front to one of the body pieces. Thread a beading needle with pale gray thread and stitch the 2 tiny silver beads in place as buttons.

6 Thread a beading needle with 2 strands of white floss and stitch the 2 white bugle beads on the wrong side of the other body piece, leaving them sticking out from the corner of the body. Then run a needle back through one of the beads and add the 2 remaining tiny white beads on the end to make the "knuckle" of the leg bone. Run the thread back through the second bead and fasten off. Thread an embroidery needle with 2 strands of red floss and bind the top end of the leg, winding the thread around the top end of the beads before fastening it off.

7 Stick the arm piece on the inside of the back body and use an embroidery needle and 2 strands of black floss to stitch the hook in place on the other side. Then align the body pieces and stitch them together with 1 strand of black floss and a small overstitch. Leave a gap at the neck and stuff the body with wisps of stuffing using a matchstick or tweezers to help you, then stitch the gap closed.

8 Thread an embroidery needle with 1 strand of black thread and stitch the body in place at the back of the head, checking the photograph to get the angle right.

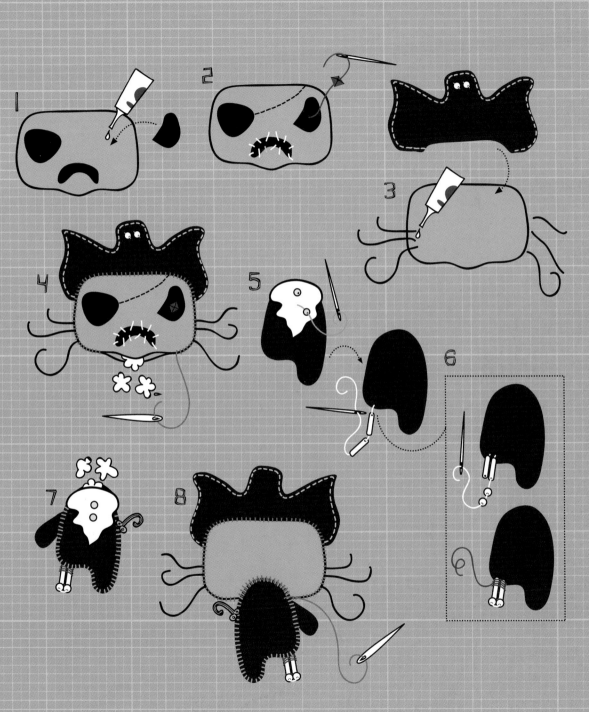

ZOMBIE FAIRY

Clap your hands if you believe in fairies! This one is small, sure, but there's something leaden about her clotted and bedraggled wings, and the teeny skull that tops her wand gives you a hint of the sickening spells she favors. She carries a needle-sharp wand, so she should be kept well out of the reach of children.

YOU WILL NEED

* 4-inch (10-cm) square of cream felt
* 4-inch (10-cm) square of dirty pink felt
* 8-inch (20-cm) square of fine white net
* Small scrap of dark gray felt
* Embroidery floss in red, cream, white, dark gray, and dirty pink
* Metallic silver embroidery floss
* 2 gray shell buttons, ½ inch (1.25 cm) in diameter
* 2 metallic pearl sequins
* 3 metallic gray bugle beads
* 2 tiny gray pearl beads
* 1 small cream bead about ¼ inch (6 mm) in diameter
* Roll of fine silver jewelry wire
* 1 embroidery needle (to make the wand), 2 inches (5 cm) long
* Tiny quantity of toy stuffing
* Embroidery needle
* Beading needle
* Pins
* Scissors
* Pencil
* Black fine-tip permanent marker
* Tracing paper
* Craft glue
* Fast-drying epoxy glue
* Matchstick or tweezers to help with stuffing

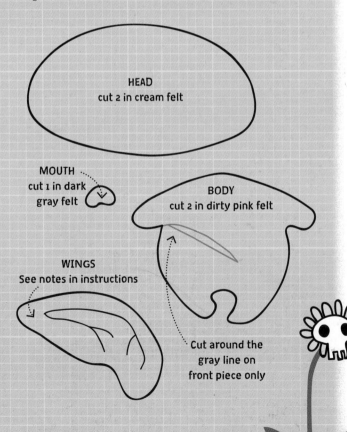

HEAD
cut 2 in cream felt

MOUTH
cut 1 in dark gray felt

BODY
cut 2 in dirty pink felt

WINGS
See notes in instructions

Cut around the gray line on front piece only

TO MAKE ZOMBIE FAIRY

1 Cut out all the felt pieces as marked, either photocopying or scanning the templates, or using tracing paper to make templates as described on page 4. Do not cut out the net for the wings. Stick the mouth onto one of the head pieces with craft glue. Thread a beading needle with 2 strands of red floss and thread on first a gray shell button and then a sequin. Stitch in place on the face to make the right eye. Repeat for the left eye.

2 Align the head pieces, thread an embroidery needle with 1 strand of cream floss, and sew them together using a small overstitch. Leave a gap at the top of the head and pad it with wisps of stuffing. Stitch the gap closed.

3 Thread an embroidery needle with 2 strands of cream floss and stitch loosely across the front body slit. It should remain slightly open. Align the body pieces, thread an embroidery needle with 1 strand of cream floss, and sew them together with a small overstitch. Leave a gap at the neck and pad the body, as with the head. Stitch the gap closed.

4 Cut a strip of net measuring about 4½ x 1 inches (11.5 x 2.5 cm). Thread an embroidery needle with 2 strands of white floss and make a line of running stitch down the center of the strip. Pull up the stitches to the width of the fairy's waist. Knot the thread, fold the strip in half, and stitch it in place to make a tutu, using the same needle and floss. Use sharp scissors to cut in some little points. Thread an embroidery needle with 2 strands of red floss and stitch some bloodstains on the left side of the tutu. Use satin stitches, slightly overlapping.

5 Cut 6 squares of net, each measuring 2 x 2 inches (5 x 5 cm). Make 2 stacks of 3 pieces each, angling the pieces slightly. Pin the pieces in each stack together. Use a pencil to trace around the wing template on each stack. Thread an embroidery needle with 2 strands of dark gray floss and backstitch the veins in the wings. Rethread the needle with 2 strands of red floss and satin stitch some blood on the left wing tip. Cut the wings out.

6 Using an embroidery needle and 1 strand of dirty pink floss, sew the body onto the back of the head. Stitch the wings to the back of the body.

7 Cut a length of the fine silver wire about 6 inches (15 cm) long and bend it into a tiny crown shape with 5 uneven points. Take one end of the skein of metallic silver floss (use all the strands) and wind it over and around the basic crown shape until it is filled in and looks solid. Cut the floss and use a dot of epoxy glue to stick it down at the back of the crown. Stitch the crown in place on Zombie Fairy's head with 1 strand of metallic silver floss.

8 Add a tiny drop of epoxy glue to the end of the embroidery needle that is to form the wand, then quickly thread on the beads, following the sequence in the photograph. Draw a skull on the larger white bead with black marker, then fix the wand through Zombie Fairy's hand and into her body with a dab of epoxy glue.

FOLKLORE ZOMBIE

DIFFICULTY RATING

The packaging is certainly attractive: pretty ornamented headwear and embroidered robe with...a splashy red pattern? That's just as well, because it helps take your attention away from the face. And the face is truly the stuff of childhood nightmares.

YOU WILL NEED

- 6-inch (15-cm) square of deep green felt
- 2-inch (5-cm) square of pale blue felt
- 2-inch (5-cm) square of red felt
- Small scraps of bright pink and black felt
- Metallic gold embroidery floss
- Embroidery floss in deep green, red, pale blue, and dark gray
- 2 tiny pearl beads
- 3 small pearl drop beads, one slightly larger than the other two
- Small quantity of dry rice
- Tiny quantity of toy stuffing
- Embroidery needle
- Beading needle
- Scissors
- Pencil
- Tracing paper
- Craft glue
- Matchstick or tweezers to help with stuffing

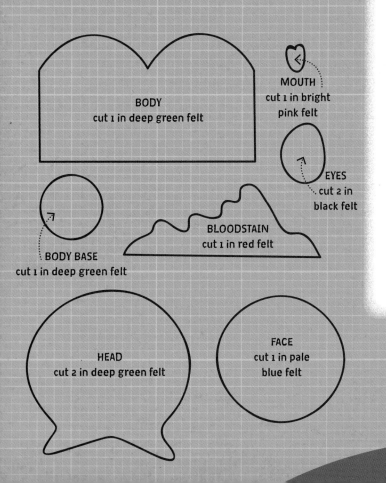

BODY
cut 1 in deep green felt

MOUTH
cut 1 in bright
pink felt

EYES
cut 2 in
black felt

BODY BASE
cut 1 in deep green felt

BLOODSTAIN
cut 1 in red felt

HEAD
cut 2 in deep green felt

FACE
cut 1 in pale
blue felt

To Make Folklore Zombie

1 Cut out all the felt pieces as marked, either photocopying or scanning the templates, or using tracing paper to make templates as described on page 4. Thread an embroidery needle with 2 strands of metallic gold floss and stitch the swirly pattern onto the front of the body piece (the left-hand panel) in backstitch, following the drawing and the photograph of the finished piece for the placement.

2 Fold the body piece in half, right-side out, align the edges, and sew them together using an embroidery needle threaded with 1 strand of deep green floss, in baseball stitch.

3 Stitch the round base piece into the bottom of the body, using the same needle and floss and a small overstitch.

4 Checking the position with the finished piece, use craft glue to stick on the red felt bloodstain at the base of the body. Thread an embroidery needle with 1 strand of red floss and stitch along the top edge of the felt in overstitch to hold the wavy shape in place.

5 Roll a scrap of paper into a funnel shape and trickle a small quantity of rice into the open top of the body to weight it. When the body is full, thread an embroidery needle with 1 strand of deep green floss and sew the top edges together with a small overstitch.

6 Glue the face in the center of one of the head pieces using craft glue. Glue the mouth and the 2 eye pieces in place on the face.

7 Thread an embroidery needle with 1 strand of pale blue floss and sew around the edge of the face with overstitch. Stitch just under the edges of the black felt at the sides of the eye pieces so that the stitches don't show on the eyes. Rethread the needle with 2 strands of red floss and embroider the patch of blood around Folklore Zombie's left eye using satin stitch and overlapping the stitches slightly to make the blood look thick and clotted.

8 Thread an embroidery needle with 2 strands of dark gray floss and stitch 4 eyelashes on each eye. The 2 central lashes are made from 2 long single stitches, end to end, and the lash at each end is made from a single stitch. Check the photography of the finished piece for placement. Sew a large cross stitch in the middle of the right eye.

9 Thread a beading needle with 1 strand of red floss and stitch one of the tiny pearl beads in place in the center of the cross on the right eye. Leave the thread loose so that the bead dangles on a loop of red floss. Knot the thread at the back of the felt, then sew the second pearl bead in place on the left eye.

TO MAKE FOLKLORE ZOMBIE [CONT.]

10 Thread a beading needle with 1 strand of pale blue floss and stitch on the pearl diadem at the top of the forehead, with the larger drop bead in the center and the smaller ones on either side of it.

11 Thread an embroidery needle with 2 strands of deep green floss. Take a short length of metallic gold floss (using all 6 strands), and twist it into 3 small loops. Place it on the inside of the second head piece and sew it on securely using the green floss. Repeat on the opposite edge of the head piece.

12 Align the head pieces and sew them together with 1 strand of deep green floss, using a small overstitch. Leave the bottom edge open and pad the head slightly with wisps of toy stuffing, using a matchstick or tweezers to help you distribute it evenly.

13 Push the top of the body slightly into the open neck of the head.

14 Thread an embroidery needle with 1 strand of deep green floss and use a small overstitch to sew the head to the body, front and back.

ZOMBIE BRIDE

DIFFICULTY RATING

Even an undead bride enjoys her special day. And here she is, draped in a tiny gray lace veil and proudly carrying a single rotting rose. Miss Havisham, eat your heart out. Or maybe she already has...

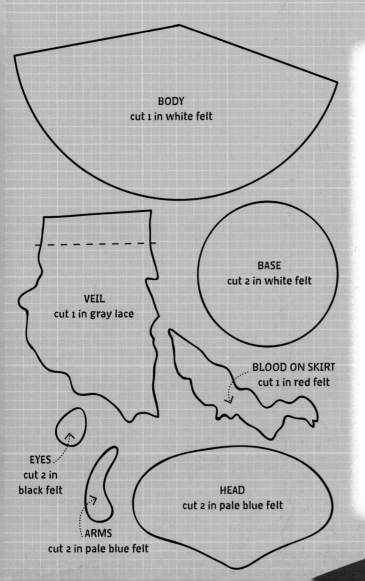

BODY
cut 1 in white felt

VEIL
cut 1 in gray lace

BASE
cut 2 in white felt

BLOOD ON SKIRT
cut 1 in red felt

EYES
cut 2 in
black felt

ARMS
cut 2 in pale blue felt

HEAD
cut 2 in pale blue felt

YOU WILL NEED

* 6-inch (15-cm) square of white felt
* 4-inch (10-cm) square of pale blue felt
* Small scraps of black and red felt
* 6-inch (15-cm) square of gray lace (choose one with a fine net base)
* Embroidery floss in dark gray, red, white, pale blue, and black
* 2 small white beads
* 6 dark gray drop beads, about ¾ inch (1.75 cm) long
* 1 tiny black artificial flower
* Tiny quantity of toy stuffing
* Small quantity of dry rice
* Embroidery needle
* Beading needle
* Scissors
* Pencil
* Tracing paper
* Craft glue
* Matchstick or tweezers to help with stuffing

TO MAKE ZOMBIE BRIDE

1 Cut out all the felt and lace pieces as marked, either photocopying or scanning the templates, or using tracing paper to make templates as described on page 4. Choose a lace with a fine net base and without too many solid motifs, otherwise you won't be able to see Zombie Bride's face.

2 Thread an embroidery needle with 2 strands of dark gray thread and stitch the bride's heart-shaped mouth on one of the head pieces using satin stitch.

3 Rethread the needle with 1 strand of red floss and embroider the line across the bottom of Zombie Bride's face in running stitch.

4 Use craft glue to stick the felt eye patches onto the face. Thread an embroidery needle with 2 strands of red floss and embroider the red patch around the left eye with satin stitch. Overlap the stitches to make the blood look thicker.

5 Thread a beading needle with 2 strands of white floss and stitch a white bead on each eye patch to make the pupils.

6 Thread a beading needle with 2 strands of pale blue floss and stitch the drop beads in place on the inner side of the second head piece to make the headdress.

7 Align the head pieces and sew them together using an embroidery needle threaded with 1 strand of pale blue floss and a small overstitch. Stitch neatly around and between the headdress beads. Leave a gap at the top of the head and pad it lightly with wisps of stuffing using a matchstick or tweezers to help you, then sew the gap closed.

8 Use the points of a pair of sharp scissors to cut a slightly ragged edge on Zombie Bride's veil and cut 1 or 2 minute holes at the lower end.

9 Thread an embroidery needle with 1 strand of pale blue floss and make a small running stitch along the top (straight) edge of the veil. Pull the thread so that the veil is gathered at the top, then knot the end.

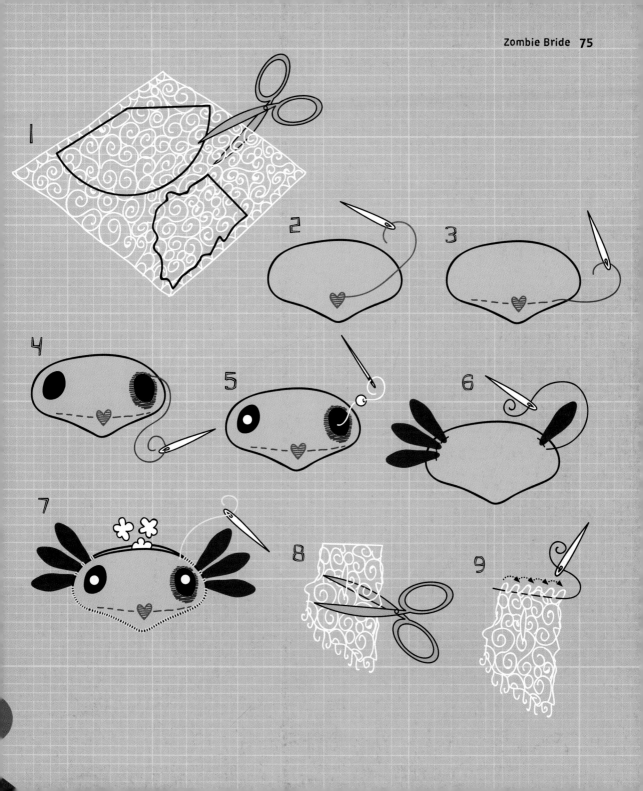

TO MAKE ZOMBIE BRIDE [CONT.]

10 Stitch the gathered top of the veil in place at the back of Zombie Bride's head using an embroidery needle and 1 strand of pale blue floss. Use the same thread to make 1 or 2 tiny stitches through the veil around the face to hold it in place.

11 Use craft glue to stick the 2 base circles together. Roll the felt body piece into a cone until the large open end is the right size to fit the base circle, and use baseball stitch to hold the edges together. Leave ¾ inch (1.75 cm) open at the top of the cone.

12 Fit the glued base into the base of the cone, thread an embroidery needle with 1 strand of white floss, and stitch the base into place in the cone using a small overstitch.

13 Roll a scrap of paper into a funnel shape, fit the narrow end into the open top of Zombie Bride's body, and pour in the rice until the body is filled up.

14 Use craft glue to stick the red felt "blood" around the front of the body, checking with the photograph for placement.

15 Use scissors to create a ragged edge along the skirt of the lace body piece, then wrap the lace around the felt body, overlapping it at the back. Thread an embroidery needle with 1 strand of pale blue floss and sew down the back of the body, stitching the lace together and securing it to the felt with small, single stitches. Work from the lower end; when you reach the open top of the cone, stitch it closed.

16 Use 1 strand of pale blue floss to sew the body onto the back of the head, checking with the photograph to get the angle right. Use craft glue to stick the arms in place at the top of the body. Use 1 strand of black floss and an embroidery needle to stitch the flower between Zombie Bride's hands.

TIP

If you can't find a black flower or gray lace, buy a packet of dark gray dye and follow the instructions to dye them in the right shades.

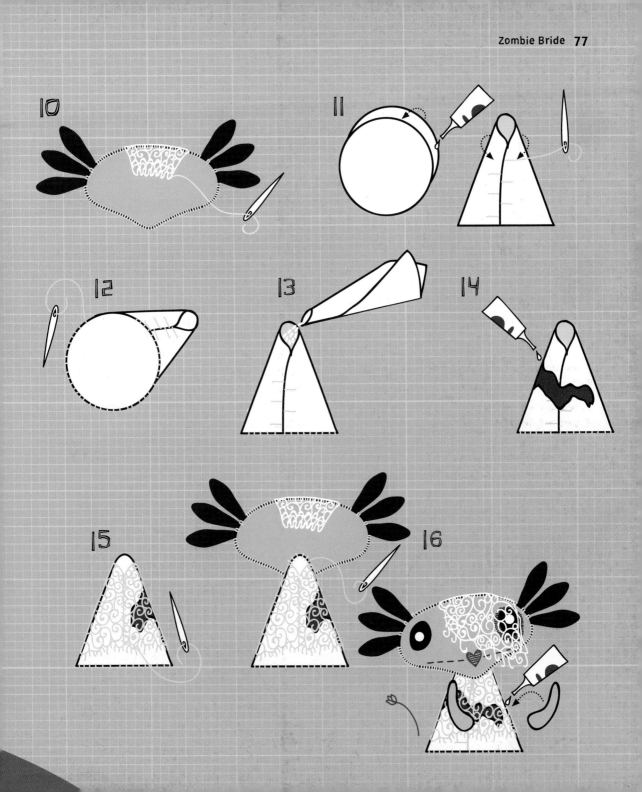

A HOME FOR YOUR ZOMBIES

Although your zombie felties are, by definition, undead, they all had to pass through a deceased stage to get to their current state. Most zombies prefer to have a coffin they can call home. To make up a zombie coffin, simply scan or color copy these templates onto paper and stick them onto a piece of firm card stock. Then fold and glue the tabs to make a cozy home.

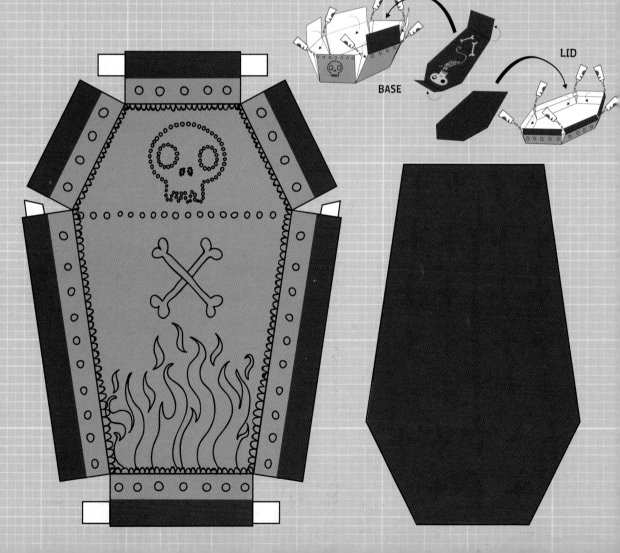

BASE

LID

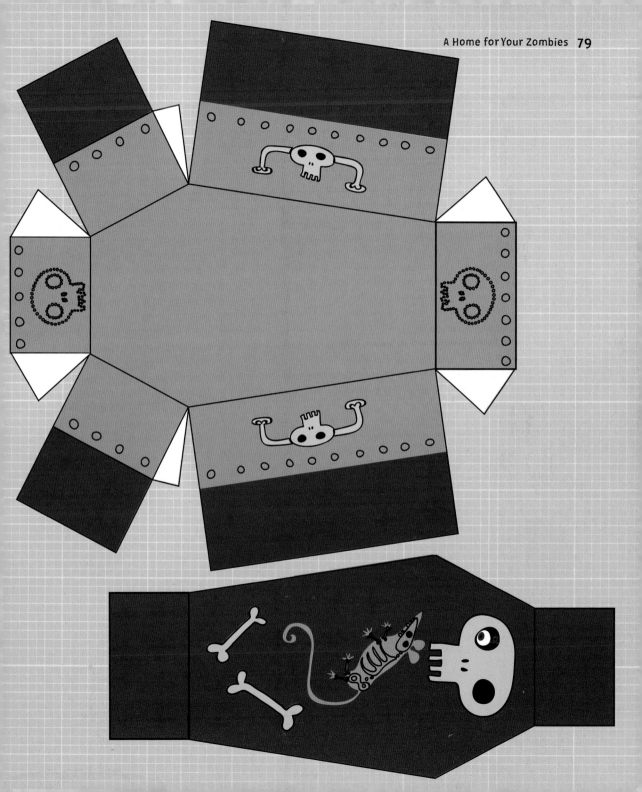

INDEX